Every Day But Tuesday

Every Day But Tuesday

Barbara Claire Freeman

OMNIDAWN PUBLISHING

OAKLAND, CALIFORNIA

2015

Cover text set in ITC Avant Garde Gothic
Interior text set in Electra Lt Std & ITC Avant Garde Gothic

Book cover and interior design by Peter Burghardt

Offset printed in the United States
by Edwards Brothers Malloy, Ann Arbor, Michigan
On 55# Heritage Book Cream White Antique
Acid Free Archival Quality Recycled Paper
with Rainbow FSC Certified Colored End Papers

Library of Congress Cataloging-in-Publication Data

Freeman, Barbara Claire.
  [Poems. Selections]
  Every day but Tuesday / Barbara Claire Freeman.
    pages ; cm
  ISBN 978-1-63243-011-3 (softcover : acid-free paper)
  I. Title.
  PS3606.R4453A6 2015
  811'.6–dc23

                              2015018145

Published by Omnidawn Publishing, Oakland, California
www.omnidawn.com   (510) 237-5472   (800) 792-4957
         10 9 8 7 6 5 4 3 2 1
         ISBN: 978-1-63243-011-3

For Brenda Hillman

Introduction

Charles Altieri

Many of the properties that make Barbara Claire Freeman's
poetry vital and challenging become visible in the very first stanza of
"Forward," the opening poem in *Every Day But Tuesday*:

> By March nothing terrible has happened.
> Only clouds, wind, stone,
> sometimes a distant engine
> before the others wake. Mud underfoot
> seems a little firmer

The opening line is decidedly different from its semantic cousins "Noth-
ing terrible happened through February," and "in March something
terrible happened." "By March" introduces the volume's concern with
temporality—with what passes and with what has to get modified continu-
ally to allow a sense of presence. This line also introduces the disturbing
unfolding of muted but persistent emotions. There is wariness about
imminent trouble. And there is the anticipation both of resistance and
of pleasure, should the poem have to confront this trouble. Here "has
happened" nicely freshens those introductory emotions because the poem
refuses the pluperfect: there is no completed past in Freeman's world but
only "a present perfectly / saturated with the future past." Yet despite, or
perhaps because of, the alignment of mind with the season, the poem
goes on to list a series of particulars, given a quiet charge by what has not
happened, and given a more voluble charge by the monosyllabic vocalics
and the taut enjambments. (As is evident in "perfectly / saturated" and
this stanza, Freeman is a leading participant in the Berkeley school of en-
jambment poetics.) In Freeman's book the individual vowels responsible
for the monosyllables seem operatic in their pronounced quasi-dramatic
internal relations. She creates situations where her audience sees these

simple objects as taking on life because sound lets them speak while protecting them from too easy absorption in our interpretive frameworks.

I will not go through all the poems in the volume noting their felicities (although someone should do it), but I want to point out how very different the second poem is, within the quiet sense of mysterious substance that pervades all of Freeman's poems. "On the Ship" continues the motif of motion developed by "Forward," with the same reliance on the mouth-filling and ear-filling and mind-filling capacities of vowels. But here the work of time is closely related to what seems an obsession with naming—probably required by the need to find something by which the ship might feel anchored:

> The channels. The breaker rolling back against
> The sand. The channels and the laugh.
> The twin. The laughter of the twin
> Rehearsed. The inlet. The little fire
> Lighting up the sand, electrical. Growing

Then, 10 lines later, the concluding sequence:

> The wet log ringed with
> Fire near the breakers. The flock of
> Sea gulls circling the pier. Wet wood
> Merged with laughter. The line. The shore.

One might complain that in this poem nothing happens beyond events of naming. But while "nothing" can be experienced simply as an abstraction, it can also come with the force of a significant discovery. The final two lines modulate from physical detail, to the figure of a "line," which combines physical detail with self-reference to the poem, to the "shore," which carries multiple meanings and, more importantly, complex feelings related to what names can and cannot do. First the "shore" widens the poem's perspective—and so incorporates all the details, reminding us that they are seen from the perspective of the boat. The "shore" may also refer metaphorically to the poem, where the lines are reconstituted into a place for imaginative dwelling. The shore marks a limit. But it also marks the direct recognition of the limit. And this direct recognition, in a poem in which nothing happens, suggests the possibility that the mind is actively learning to accept that it is responsible for this nothing. Accepting this responsibility in turn gives presence to the other side of the line, the liminal threshold where "shore" hovers between the landscape seen from a distance and the distance-making powers of the mind at work up-close and intimate.

My favorite poem in the book is probably "Datebook." This presents a marvelous meditation on the senses as sources of dialogue that eventually allows the full embrace of whatever "I" can come to represent through the powers exercised within the poem. But this poem is too long and complicated to deal with here. So I will turn to another terrific poem that seems to me to best represent the spirit of the volume. This poem is in the final section of "The Gift":

> evidence wrapped in silk
> air thin above peaks we can't

> vi.

> see as when
> speaking in tongues
> we wonder if

> hunting birds would dive or head east
> if refusing water mattered
> if the snow would keep

> never telling
> about the clearing a mile further
> so very like this moment

We might notice first how Freeman extends the basic structural principle of the middle section of short poems, "#343," into the dynamics of an individual lyric. "#343" not only enjambs lines of poetry but experiments with a kind of enjambment among specific lyrics. Most of the individual poems constituting this section can be read as commenting on or extending what had become present in the previous poem. So this middle section offers a dialogue in which readers are invited to pick various elements of the previous poem because they bear directly on what the successor poem confronts. Yet it is only some of the pieces that continue, so the destructive and reconstructive aspects of time are on stage. The same struggle applies to internal relations in "The Gift" as the poem struggles not to lose individual moments to the sense of time and loss built into any sequential movement.

This final section brilliantly picks up the motif of evidence, submitting it to complex indeterminacies within what still seem simple concrete observations. The subject of "never telling" is probably "we." But it could also be the birds or the snow, depending on the kind of clearing to which one decides the poem is referring. The point is not simple indeterminacy but the registering of multiple possibilities for imagining the nature and role of "clearing." Grammar functions as a semantic and dramatic operator, a recurrent trait in Freeman's poetry.

Then we have to ask how the clearing a mile away can be "so very like this moment." What is the clearing posed by "this moment"? And why does the similarity matter for our affective grasp of the situation? I suspect that appreciating the force of these questions is more important than any tentative efforts we might make toward answering them. Yet "very like" calls out for dramatic analysis, as if "this moment" were both worth celebrating and worth fearing, since its momentariness is so insistently stressed. "This moment" may be clear because the speaker accepts how wondering can take the place of seeing. Clarity then resides in the poem's accepting the limits of knowledge; its questions are muted exclamations that bypass the need for indicative confirmation. "[V]ery like" becomes a hope for likeness that will diminish the threats posed by the force of time. Relations among sounds are crucial to the formation of such clearings, since they define forceful spatial relations that do not depend on anything but their capacity to help us recognize how different modes of syntax modify our sense of being.

Every Day But Tuesday offers the intricate suggestiveness of Symboliste poetry in the straightforward musical language of objectivists like Lorine Neidecker. Here the actual object is the material force that allows us to feel the weight of a fluid world finding complex substance through mobilizing all the resources of grammar. It is not much of an exaggeration to say that Freeman treats both sonic effects and grammatical complexities as the basic personages in her poems. The result is a sensual volubility that treats as a cause of satisfaction the realization that objects cannot appease the hungers of mind. There is a constant dawning of aspects as the mind follows traces made by previous decisions. The poems construct a stable home for the mind in the grammatical structures that underlie our capacities for making sense. Lost in time but found within the recuperable background of lyric space, in Freeman's poems time proves as fluid and insubstantial as the contents of thought.

Charles Altieri is the author of *Wallace Stevens and the Demands of Modernity* and *Reckoning With Imagination: Wittgenstein and Literary Theory*, Cornell University Press.

CONTENTS

A Particular Kind of Giving

Forward

By March nothing terrible has happened.
Only clouds, wind, stone,
sometimes a distant engine
before the others wake. Mud underfoot
seems a little firmer

this time around, the breeze
a long quotation.
Shifting banks of words rise like steam
in darkness or under water. Miles
from the nearest whatever, at

the very moment description advances
into daylight, yellowing wood
from a recent overhaul disappears
over the ridge. But by then
a fence was falling or a woman

had dismantled it. Just seconds ago
in the new climate, rain so dense
it took my breath. All arrivals
postponed, no one has been
back since. Latest reports

show that months are slowing down
a little more each year. Another
cool day tomorrow with morning
frost along the road. I'm always
the last to know but I hear it's closed—
the river, the forest, this way.

On The Ship

The channels. The breaker rolling back against
The sand. The channels and the laugh.
The twin. The laughter of the twin
Rehearsed. The inlet. The little fire
Lighting up the sand, electrical. Growing
Underneath. The pier. The laughter of
The other, unheard. Piles of wood
Rolling back against the pier. The fire.
The water. The inlet. The sunset
Giving way to malice between twins.
The twins. The wet log ringed with
Fire near the breakers. The flock of
Seagulls circling the pier. Wet wood
Merged with laughter. The line. The shore.

Parable

one year black grains one year white
one year water fills with sand

one year glass, a curtain of glass
one year calls to prayer unanswered

we drew a line in the sand
then there were two years

our neighbor harbored devils
hills came into focus, it had rained

one year erased
redder than wind one year

the promised end of days
thirst and sun, the distant

no longer distant year
we saw ourselves

motionless where dunes were
once fire once before

the bearded man stretched out an arm
pointed in several directions

offering the possibility of
one year following shade

Evening On The Other Channel

Smell of lime from this place we made
out of a villager's blood and limbs
of castaways. Is there slant rain?
No, a brief meltdown followed
by reversals, chainlink, honeysuckle.
None of us can get to the cavern
under the temple where
we went to watch the monster,
only one example
of a year marked on calendars
destroyed by water. I looked it up once.
There were people here before us,
now it's all electric torches, scarlet wheels.

Detail

Unslide a door you're not allowed
to shut, unlock a box
in which the music's dusk, the kept
does rise and fade the sky, the mist
in little drops does fill the air
and in this way another sky
dissolves, layered clouds spin past
a minor cleft the sun undoes,
voices after dark have depth enough.
They are our blue glass chime,
hour after hour, one door and the next
transported from a major key until
each motion seems exact, the same.

Why I Am Not A Critic

Nothing self-evident could be false, nor was it possible
to restore an abandoned picnic ground in a public park
closed for lack of funds. Barren states grew larger.
A high-ranking official ordered animated fireworks
to appear upon an immense, golden scrim;

water emptied from a manmade lake
into a history no metaphor could match.
As night progressed bamboo gave way
piece by piece to paper. These multitudes failed
to amuse and the sky, ever volatile, took on

more complex roles. The result was rapture,
then panic—keeping memory separate
from explanation's clouded landscapes or crystal bells.
When a bottle takes the place of breath
and frees a trapped verb, souls at war and relatives

joined to animals become a theme: a leader passes
through his subjects with the ease of wind.
On New Year's Eve a select few formed a circle
and whispered a secret phrase into the next ear.
Traveling until the message no longer

resembled the original, the first person to unscramble
it won a gadget that measured angles. The amusement
did not dull even after diverse permutations had spun out;
no one who left through the service entrance ever wished
to enter through another. Meanwhile sovereigns

laid down scraps; the syntax and mumbo-jumbo
peculiar to consciousness tossed out emotions
like so much confetti, a sort of cuckoo nest
embedded in your frontal lobe. Yet it was precisely
this question the faculties were asking themselves:

they were not entirely wrong in believing
their purpose was to turn a profit every minute.
Not a line could be authorized nor a chair endowed
without provosts being forced to reassess priorities
and account for rivalries—when remembered,

they faded as might the profile of a ruined suburb
if you turned away from the reader terrified
that what she was reading might suddenly be.

Downtown

The month was like that, neatly slashed—
Tuesday, wisteria, damaged rhyme.
For me it's less about the latest plan than weather
Added to whatever Armageddon's rising faster than.
I know it's not our river emptied but a network
Narrowing the search for meters driving
Motorists to double-park in red zones,
Vacant lots. So let a narrative begin:
This March the seventh bookstore closed, we celebrated
Easy credit in an age of atriums and glue
Before another storm came through I read
Online "No woman rules me while I live" (Antigone),
Returned to where there once was something called
Now overgrown with poppies, framed by green.

The Given

i.

Maybe at the end
an interruption   If that, then
flesh survives in peat
the members won't miss   By which time
one must imagine the image unmade
Didn't we learn from the previous song
how yellow lingers in flowering weeds?

If the moon wakes them they will be happy
I was at the summit, I was alone

ii.

It doesn't seem like a gift
the soon to-be-willfully offered
sleet, the sky

Sing it again in a different octave
Sing until your name finds you another

iii.

Arrangement in a system
sliding back   it's there and then

All morning I waited for no one
Something told me the trial was just a walk from
the waterfall but there is no waterfall no

one here wants to talk about glaciers

iv.

Debt happens like this—
three same necklaces, red mother-of-pearl
at dusk   the dusky noon

v.

the simplest form implies
as if what was given could be given back

vi.

Give it to
Give it to the field of white poppies
The reward leans
Against a dark the dark leans on
Sometimes night is long enough
Richer now coming as it did just once

Sorbitol For Sugar

We can hear any number of people
talk about the water tower,
the rain battering windows,
how the plot had to be given up,
replaced. They said
clouds would decrease in the late afternoon.
I wonder where substitutes are hidden.
Rubylight. Ice chips. Pieces
missing from the ornamented vase.

But it's not that simple.
In the jewelry-box nicknamed "Dora's,"
there's a tiny dictionary, bookmarked.
"Antithesis," brother to "prosthesis,"
sister to "synthesis," divorces Theseus,
murders Odysseus, fucks Narcissus,
for years Freud wore a prosthetic jaw.
Quick! Find the replacement.
Faster, faster.

Hologram

near the quays
      wet lightless
  day thickened

tides dwarfed
      this low mechanical
  hum

west of here
      someone left
  black ewes

and a ram
      tied to the wreck
  another   pale as flesh

beneath the marsh
      a person almost
  rose up   failed again

crouched   chipped a little
      through trees
  icicles

open
      in our hands
  but ahead

another now is
        standing
    though barely alive

in empty space
        and curving lines
    heavier than

the figure
        floating facedown
    an early haze

yellow   yellowest

Every Day But Tuesday

It was when a song in the form of a question
meant for anyone who might have taken part
in conversation overheard by strangers
made clear the day before was like today, less
shade aligning fields within an open sky.
If my chronology is right it still could happen—
adolescents skating near a lake realize
the hum they heard more like a quatrain than
a warning antecedent to a message sent
was where the ice grew thinnest, near a present
soon-to-be outsourced. Their voices break
up under pressure, address a speaker
rather than speak through her—have you missed
a second, two or twenty thousand
ways to measure those who see themselves
twinned by shadows painted near a manmade lake.
That was when whole days went drifting,
blackouts served as an example, bells hidden
under pavement crowned with weeds derived
power from each failure: why not let the kids
believe quiet comes from multiplying questions,
alter headlights in a glare that only happens once?
Strangers made more strange by waiting
hear one too many versions of a theme
put in motion as the drone begins it is
the blue and crimson coloring the bronze,
maybe a bomb threat or a demonstration,
doesn't matter how long sound takes to travel
while helicopters illuminate the fences
bordering the lake. Tones deepen,

icons on this evening's news repeat

that opalescent streaks across the sky touched ice.

No one expects a fist closed in defiance

although some parts may yet go on for years.

Begin a sequence every time alarms resound,

this is tomorrow and the sun

seems certain as horizons, day creeps down

where lakes divide one body from another

green hills open, subordinates

watch afternoon become a night-child

shuttling back from private space

to public damage, how else could it happen—

separate lines cross grids that never quite appear

within these memories of lived election: the pond,

lagoon, more empty billboards resting

or displacing sixty watts twelve chords away.

It might be June on Sunday centuries before

the next trimester, each term's a sentence

during leap-year families extend

connections no one asks how many different

systems make nearly perfect figure-eights

wherever ice holds doors click shut,

light replaces dusk the skaters morning in.

#343

Then: gone.
What was she thinking?
A perfect copy,
that's what she thought.
That's wrong—

it's green, not blue—
there's time enough
to make a landscape disappear
along a riverbank
where the water is dark
and smooth and very cold.

She who listens
hard does not see
the gesture of terror
structured like machines
waiting to be nourished

where agents space traffic
as typesetters space type,
lettering made visible
as it's done away with—
faded a little less,
transmitted only twice.

Night was an absent river, tone
shuttling from the radio tower
gathering and receiving
precise continuous notes
difficult to separate

from dropped signals
animals had warned us of, anytime
minutes following unpredictable
groupings, before a night backlit
blacker than any gathering.

But backward to a night
where nothing moves
what she heard was mostly
"always dusk here, what have you
got there in your hand?"

Near the forest
wind picks up speed—
only the most indistinct sounds
reach a listener for whom the question
has become superfluous, fields
of petrified wood, not far
from where entire populations

should arrive any day now
sometime after winter but not too late,
I'll explain all this if you come—
interrupting a gesture gives it power
when there aren't enough night

hours and each season models
a collapsing present underlined in red,
interrupting laughter without lungs,
the rustle of fallen leaves across
an unimportant path.

Now the image is
identical to its flames, but not
for us, a starlight shot
through with reflections
so close there was no telling

how many had been chosen
or by whom. This is how
we must speak around a fire
that isn't fully real, daughters
laid next to narratives set
out along the floor—

Beneath the shadowy lines
a guardian waits, expecting
you to interrupt that gesture, make
legible, now and then
while the sky is white, still

now and then a gesture
expects its guardian to reinvent
and cite, so deep in the forest
"pine trees" are the only answer
quiet enough to hear beneath
underbrush the wind comes in.

The copy machine will stop
making copies only when
the copy machine will stop
not on the last
day but on the very last

day of a winter where
mostly the weather was fine,
without any breaks
in a present perfectly
saturated with the future past.

Even at night darkness settles
around Gliwice, the last wooden tower
full of leaves and bits of song
patched onto branches
standing upright as if on two legs

so many legs in a row
following tunnels hidden
in plants of which it's said
they found solvent where
nightshade should have been
chalkwhite, bonewhite, crystal.

In the middle forest is a distance
that rises through summer
asleep and seeming.
There is not even one
unpainted canvas or clock

that measures the duration of colors
as they flash. There is
no thought here of
so very small a glimmer
passed on in the night to others
which from the remotest distance
the forest takes back.

What is to come but the ladder
twigs and the wish and little
drops, some rusted wire
in the field where streams
still are. At the next gate

nothing opens. Those forbidden
to stop hear a language made
from squares speak something
other than itself. Near the hill
no one recalls, this is where a latch
should be, black asterisks and

later someone says there was no animal—
they are little things from boarded-up places
now all but visible—an arm,
thumb, sacred text, a pond
splayed in every direction

as day follows day and metal bins
extend the danger sign beyond the road.

One year, then forty-eight, then
a plateau with seven pine trees
we're told we must keep on our right,
vineyards leading to a ridge, hardly
discernible trail near boulders

becoming less and less symbolic,
visas for unknown countries, imagined
ships, real captains—
he'll end up too far north
beneath a series of vertical planes,
stalks heavy with black grapes.

No different from the collective
hurtling past suns, one
at the end, another at the junction,
a third implying anthems insufficiently
arranged, as if in a haze of leaves

a door within the forest shut.
People whisper. A people's music
whispers, an obsolescence emptier
than melody. "Together we
see this skeleton displayed like an X?"
Yes, these were their teeth, some notes.

But where in all that noise
sweeping over the masts and towers
is a transmitter powerful enough to entertain
witnesses who hold their breath and hear
mostly tires on the road and cars

passing. First the noise and then
the breeze and then the shade and then
the hum. Then nothing but the
then of unrecorded voices without sound.

I think the bells have stopped
tolling the same note again and again
but something else is mimicking the sound of gunfire
on nights when there's no wind
tell it to the wind. When there's no moon //

A book closes. A calendar
closes. The people still inside
turn their faces toward a declaration
made by no one, nearly audible
in the middle of a darkened afternoon.

It's because
of broken signals and the day
lasting longer than its hours, though
never so slowly as when X replaced Y
leaving gaps that may soon merge
with darker air.

Mechanical landscapes may also
accelerate or vanish at
the simple motion of a hand,
prescribed by a sequence of events
replaced. Now there are

many journeying through night, stars
whitened by sunlight, falling trees
spread thin, enlarged
the way a negative is.
Either continued silence or
many journeying through night, stars.

New images arrive each winter
streaming past trees that make sense
to us now. I wonder if our asterisks
will matter, and if so when? Outside
the river is flowing swiftly toward a tentative

conclusion. It's still early in the season
thus evening brings us to an antique place
that is a kind of ammunition dump, a celebration
sequestered near roots
whose story must be told before it can occur.

Look it's raining again, we
reach out to strangers waiting
on the stairs, in the corridor, hall,
wanting to see a plant become another,
an animal become a different animal

still wet along the ramparts but
there's no one else for miles, skyway
stretching overhead resembles
animated passages from last season
or century that cannot yet be seen through.

Some days the forest is blue-green and
how would the copy look
if color no longer mattered, some days
disappear so rapidly they can be glimpsed
only where sky joins sky

and a receding horizon cuts
the blind spots out. Sometimes she thinks
copies are machines that must be disassembled carefully,
exact replicas of evergreens that aren't merely

along a path beneath the echoing pines
a gathering waits, afraid that she
will reproduce that gesture
now and then while the dirt is still
wet, still there, and then

holds us motionless
longer than particles of sun
on stones these patterns will repeat,
pyre-like, derivative, its signature
stretching for miles and a page.

What We Meant By Alms

Prequel

As if the lamp left on demands the better part
of streets in which I find myself

up to a point, a body with more roles to play
now joined by a third I can't see through

recurrent whiteness glowing up ahead
made of hours in the temporary way, they rise

half-shining, offering more reasons not to count
how far small drops of water travel then

contract along this path it seems
I've spiraled back as chance

subjects no one has seized before broadcast
the glassed-in sky, the transference of night.

On The Ship

Out past the blue wave
The break in the shoreline. The break
In the wave. The person is sleeping.
A break in the ship. The berth and
The floating. Up by blue waves.
Up by the blue wave a person is
Sleeping, the raft and the ship.
A slip in the shoreline. The break
And the berthing. Up past the wave.
The raft and the person. The shoreline.
The berth. The berth and the mooring.
The shoreline is waiting. A break-in
Is waiting. The raft and the ship.
A break in the fogbank. The shoreline.

Untitled

here is a rock
or a line through a name

here is glass
or a curtain of dust

here is July
an altered object

kindling here
the letter X

is amplified sound
or a page on a screen

a speaker recorded
a message here

here is tobacco
the exchange of signs

promises goods
perhaps causing pain

here is a word we cannot
and here is the furnace

where we feel rich
the landfall the plant

here is July
our meat

here is laughter
the match the lighter

the fluid an army
the blink of an eye

still looking for noon
in other people's tents

here is smoke
what we meant by alms

here is the bonfire
here its redder than

The Gift

i.

not "yes" exactly
but mountains and haze

not "maybe" either

all sorts of beginnings
until the wind blows

one day a whitened future

ii.

would have rubbed
twigs together

collapsed beside
whatever we went looking for
but there was no

above the tree line
too high for landslides
stars once were

iii.

what might have been
but was not

stolen   the adjective
"unstained"
and useless   three articles

we carried to a hole
and buried under rocks

having nothing
to compare our hunger to

iv.

each day we must give a little more
as if it's better to
crush the fingers of one hand

when darkness darkens
the afternoon hardly begun
one of us must

compel the god to return
hammers   pick-axe   flowering

time doing what time does
wailing upon the ridge

v.

the trick was
to awaken it again and again
one sentence after another

failing that
our first witness says
even abandoned
the thing given possesses the giver

evidence wrapped in silk
air thin above peaks we can't

vi.

see as when
speaking in tongues
we wonder if

hunting birds would dive or head east
if refusing water mattered
if the snow would keep

never telling
about the clearing a mile further
so very like this moment

Symbolic Logic

In the middle of a reservoir
in the middle of a drought
hoping to avoid the silent hour
whose ruddy afterglow suggests

an event that hasn't yet occurred.
As if I could tell you our story—
brittle days and only one night
but there is no story in that. Still
the captive is unable to report correctly

details captured during her journey.
Blistersea. Eardrum. Scabsurge.
I was absent twice. I wish I could say
it made a difference but it didn't.
When she says "blood orange"
I hear "tympanum." It goes on like that—

so much work building a beginning
where everything is hooked up.
Meanwhile the interviews have started.
When she gets back it will be too late.
This country was nothing before it had a King.

The Ship Found

The ship found a theme and swerved. We might
find a star here. Wasted breath or
breath cut by rain. Praise it,
it's not the wind that
is wrong. Either the fire casts a
shadow or it won't. At the cutwater
a pale wave. Rode it like breakers shearing
through the night. That's how it works here. Afraid
the wind will end tonight? Always like this,
gone from the start. Friends almost
lied here. Can I say it? You
can't hear what I hear. So enter lack.
I've prayed too long and should stay here.

Sequel

Where the river we are coming back from turns
blue-black, off-black, or paler than

the shapes that are tomorrow's offspring,
voices nearly close enough sung

again from singing what they ought to say.
There public songs evaporate by night,

privatize a space whose lines converge
into a park becoming equal. The hum

of frequencies within dry air
that moves a day too soon may also signal

anywhere change presents a conversation
waiting to be heard, a yes-in-motion,

transient mutual regard, as many shocks
as moments flashing, gathered stones.

Heraclitus

The colonist finds a path home.
Come in, come in. Welcome
back. The six blue
pills we stare at stare back.

Everyone agrees a job worth doing once
must be done again, until by accident
we fetch forks and paring knives, a relish dish,
condiments, those twisted blades

men use. Sitting down
to a vegan meal, everything we touch
turns to ice. My friends stop eating.
Now they are asleep. Weeds, really.

Hologram

unwrapped
    the bandage chewed
  clean   late evening

or last evening
    narratives turn
  west   blue mountain

foothill   plain
    the way dirges move
  over there

low and damp
    weeds frame
  tomorrow's windfall

cobbled   uncobbled
    we bring wooden spoons
  mud   salt

virus   a few drops
    of black rain
  beyond the river

white voyage
    over water
  not the river

but what floats there
      Sirius' light
   cold currents

barely move
      along tracks
   sliding past

we moved burial
      grounds north
   bones hauled

toward the jetty
      we imagined   saw
   coiled roots   vines

amulets
      an orange our moon
   counting waves

by hand
      the fog pours in

Draft

But it is this shoreline at dusk
now sea-green now slightly gray, prosodic
wreckage intended to be seen
as the tail of kites, rulers, or wingless birds

whose names are found discrepant.
But this dictation while night breaks down
like an impossible sea surging toward
the station we are on, the at-risk coast.

Stranger, leave the mainland to itself—
compared to "daylight" in those first two lines
you are the relic taken up, apart.
Before the laughtrack starts, we welcome
the outer island: half-wild and half-dross.

The Ship Found

I could begin again with curtains, still
grateful something in the distance turns
whatever is approaching back,
a temporary lull, the sun seems like
it's frozen in the West. Another truer way
might be to translate shades
of silver-blue or silver in the field
before increasing dusk objects,
cements skyline to sky. At 5 p.m.
I'll finish the incision while our ship does nothing,
it is always the same rising and falling
from a distance about to be replaced
by next year's annotation, air in sheets.

Blindness And Hindsight

A prophet appears with word

of an island lying behind us.
Embossed columns divide yesterday's

season from its counterpart
and appear almost blue as they shed

perspective on whatever drifts
past. It is terribly cold.

Yet the disorder that gives a face
to the hurricane's eye is not one you can

see—you always knew you could
see, but the original face

was never there. Deathly?
No, not yet. The murder becomes

suicide where the castaway turns
the weapon of their language

on herself. You believe thoughts
can be heard. Amid posthumous lives

kept hidden by failing tidal systems,
every survivor has a story

three times as wide and three times
as deep as the previous one, over there.

Datebook

If you stand here you can see the new
that looks down to the sky within the river,
a narrative just undertaken
though no sound reaches the figure
outside. Scores collect and dissipate
like oxygen entangled in water, seem
near except for silver things
that move at night. A third apparition
backs up, stops again—same
hazard, logarithm, shadow under leaves
caught in a net, though briefly.
It's been raining off and on for years
and names we have replaced begin to soften
pauses unalloyed by any other
that as rumored is a little dark.
If you listened you could hear themes passing
as each intended note falls off across
late afternoon glare, gives way
to artificial measures, but that's
not really right. There are other exits
without doors or awnings, adjacencies
whose parts align and then, as if deliberately,
shut down although this would be as good
a place as any not to forget
the first suspension of a muted chord
on a day that strangely makes no difference

whether the delay is temporary or meant
to wind up somewhere else.
What happens next concerns no one at all—
strangers barely notice quiet breaking
intermittently calm waters narrow
via intermediate trees reflected
beneath an oxidizing sky. Yes,
but now they're listening. The message
burned into what you'd thought of as
yourself has been revised too many times
to offer news about the world in which
its words are set, parallel constructions
whose lesson is obscure. There must be
compelling reasons for this silence
coming from the hills, a voluntary recall
made simple by the loss of detail
"musical phrases perfectly sum up,"
recognizable enough to parse
cadences fed by others to the wind.
Something beside stasis keeps repeating
threes and fours within a blue uncertain
whether off-beats count as one or many
when you'd expected absence. Gleams
of sun move closer to their passage
through slant light, interrupted
by apostrophes that turn the work

of termination into just another missing
"G" referring back to yellow prisms:
you will not be departing.
The pattern comes to seem no more than
nightfall just ahead, a soundscape
in which running water echoes speech-acts
but not one single written page becomes
unutterably blank, no song cycle, trace,
nor any humming sound made tuneable
by greetings you would have slept
a long time not to hear. Add
banners, birdcall, things with limbs—
the next a hundred yards behind the peace
of night dividing night as it is dreamed, yet close
to ice plants, obligatory storms, broken phones
in the disappearing half-line shuttling
back and forth across landings there's no point
trying to escape. Someone might make whiteness
rise from the river on days you thought
were all alike become like music, but still
you gaze into a surface that gives back
nothing at all, not even silver-gray
or purple settling in the evening sun.
The problem isn't whether to disguise
a faded subject but is one of seeing:
if you ever were and whose you might

have been. Past, passing, or to come —
is it still possible to be this question
lengthened by recurrent phrases
mostly empty burdens that adhere,
combine, unable to ignore
a riddle you're not sure of having heard?
Where first-person vagrant answers
such as "No one owns me" or "I belong to x"
modify a body nested within clauses,
repeat, exactly, what was on the page,
the river spills into a second
of which you are the paraphrase.
The curve continues what led to it —
three breaths, three vocables, a single zero
prompted by verbs that would have minimized
how hard it is to enter the same stream
twice without a speaker. Someone says
but that's not really more than color wheels
combine uncomplimentary shades
which do not matter, water rearranges
sundials, missiles, bells, a wayside bridge
across the sound the cascade brings. Shock
waves, years of them, confusing voices
in the dusk with rhythms found in transit,
retrieve an antecedent louder now than any
that came before. If you stand here

long enough to see this bright thing promised
you will not remember how it felt
unless the presence of a larger series
emerges naked from within the word "to give"
until it's ended. Until it's ended and another
free to act as if alone disturbs
mid-sentence shifts you'd thought were
numerous enough to seem an evening sky
you saw again, the object of a pause held still
without regard to who or what you are.
Record not having any law to follow
slashes softer than a comma, break
so slight it hardly lengthens uneven distributions
there's no use trying to forbid the possibility
of choosing rather than the choice itself,
and all the sad etceteras of lines
replied to merely by continuing
a scale distended so there might be less
you'd given up, sketched in, or held against
indifferences running through too thin, I said.

Notes:

"Forward" collages and paraphrases occasional lines from *Flow Chart* by John Ashbery.

"#343" was inspired by Kafka's letters and *Parables*. The title refers to the poem by Emily Dickinson numbered #343, and pirates her stanza pattern.

In "Datebook" the line "Made simple by the loss of detail" is from the poem "Directive" by Robert Frost.

Acknowledgments and Dedications

Thanks to the editors of the following publications for publishing some of the poems in this book: *A Public Space, Agriculture Reader, Berkeley Poetry Review, The Boston Review, The Colorado Review, Crazyhorse, Denver, Quarterly, Forklift, Ohio, Jacket, Lana Turner: A Journal of Poetry and Opinion, The Laurel Review, Maggy, The Offending Adam, The Seattle Review, Volt: A Magazine of the Arts, The Volta, Washington Square Magazine,* and *Wave Composition.*

#343 appeared as a limited-edition chapbook from Chapvelope Press, 2014. My gratitude to Andrew Wessels.

Special thanks to Rusty Morrison, Ken Keegan, Peter Burghardt, and everyone at Omnidawn.

"Datebook" is for Ben Lerner.
"Every Day But Tuesday" is for Geoffrey G. O'Brien.
"The Gift" is for Jeff Clark.
"The Given" is for Forrest Gander.
"Hologram" is for Brian Teare.
"#343" is for Judith Butler.
"Parable" is for Amanda Nadelberg.

About the Author

Barbara Claire Freeman is a literary critic and professor of literature who has recently turned her full attention to writing poetry. She is the author of *The Feminine Sublime: Gender and Excess in Women's Fiction* (University of California Press), among many other works of literary theory and criticism. Formerly an Associate Professor of English at Harvard, she teaches creative writing and poetics in the Rhetoric Department at UC Berkeley.

Incivilities, her first collection of poems, was published by Counterpath Press in 2009; a chapbook, *St. Ursula's Silence*, was published by Instance Press in 2010; *#343* was published by Chapvelope Press in 2014. Selections from these collections won the *Boston Review*/Discovery Prize and the Campbell Corner Prize (Sarah Lawrence College).

Photo credit: Chloe Apfel

Every Day But Tuesday
by Barbara Claire Freeman

Cover text set in ITC Avant Garde Gothic
Interior text set in ITC Avant Garde Gothic & Electra Lt Std

Book cover and interior design by Peter Burghardt

Offset printed in the United States
by Edwards Brothers Malloy, Ann Arbor, Michigan
On 55# Heritage Book Cream White Antique
Acid Free Archival Quality Recycled Paper
with Rainbow FSC Certified Colored End Papers

Publication of this book was made possible in part by gifts from:
Robin & Curt Caton
Deborah Klang Smith
John Gravendyk
Barbara White, Trustee, Leaves of Grass Fund

Omnidawn Publishing
Oakland, California
2015
Rusty Morrison & Ken Keegan, senior editors & co-publishers
Gillian Olivia Blythe Hamel, managing editor
Cassandra Smith, poetry editor & book designer
Peter Burghardt, poetry editor & book designer
Melissa Burke, poetry editor & marketing manager
Sharon Zetter, poetry editor, book designer, & grant writer
Liza Flum, poetry editor
RJ Ingram, poetry editor
Juliana Paslay, fiction editor
Gail Aronson, fiction editor
Josie Gallup, publicity assistant
Sheila Sumner, publicity assistant
Kevin Peters, warehouse manager
Janelle Bonifacio, office assistant
Abbigail Baldys, administrative assistant